W9-BSL-930

Two Special Valentines

by Janet McDonnell
illustrated by Jodie McCallum

created by Wing Park Publishers

CP CHILDRENS PRESS ®
CHICAGO

Library of Congress Cataloging-in-Publication Data

McDonnell, Janet, 1962-
  Two special valentines / by Janet McDonnell ; illustrated by Jodie
McCallum : created by Wing Park Publishers.
    p.   cm. — (Circle the year with holidays)
  Summary: Kevin and James are so involved in making each
other's valentines that they almost stop being friends. Includes
handicrafts.
  ISBN 0-518-00692-4 (library binding)
  [1. Valentine's Day—Fiction.   2. Friendship—Fiction.   3.
Handicraft.]   I. McCallum, Jodie, ill.   II. Wing Park Publishers.
III. Title.   IV. Title: 2 special valentines.   V. Series.
PZ7.M478436Tw   1994
[E]—dc20   93-37097
                                                               CIP
                                                               AC

Two
Special Valentines

Every day at 1:30, Mrs. Fisher's class has free time. Some kids go to the reading corner. Other kids pick the science center.

But not Kevin and James. They always pick the creation station. That's where the paper, scissors, crayons and glue are. Kevin and James love to create. They make the most wonderful things.

One day they made space helmets and a control panel. They pretended they were astronauts on a space shuttle.

Another time they made vines and hung them up to look like a jungle. Then they made maps and a compass so they could find their way out.

So it's no wonder that, when Mrs. Fisher told the class Valentine's Day was only a few days away, Kevin and James each had the same, secret idea.

"I'm going to make James the most amazing valentine ever," thought Kevin.

"Just wait until Kevin sees the valentine I make for him," thought James.

On the way home from school, James thought of ideas for his valentine. Maybe I'll draw pictures of Kevin's favorite things. I'll make a fire truck, and a shark, and a baseball player. And I'll have to use glitter. Kevin loves glitter.

When he finished the drawings, James
looked around for glitter. But there was none
to be found. "I'll take you to the store later,"
Mom promised.

At that same moment, Kevin was busy planning his valentine for James. He sat at the kitchen table with a pencil and paper, thinking of ideas. "I know what I'll do," he thought. "I'll make a big spring out of paper. Then I'll put a heart on the end so when James opens the card, the heart will jump out at him! But how will I keep the card from popping open too soon?"

Just then, the phone rang. It was James.

"Hi, Kevin. Want to come over to play?" he asked.

"No, thanks," said Kevin. "I'm busy."

"What are you doing?" asked James.

"I can't tell you. I'm just busy, that's all," said Kevin. "I have to go. Bye."

James hung up the phone. He folded his arms and frowned. "Fine," he said. "If Kevin doesn't want to play with me, I don't want to play with him."

Later that day, James went to the store to buy glitter. He tried to forget how mad he was at Kevin, but it was hard. Still, he would finish the valentine. After all, it was almost done.

As James and his mom were leaving the store, who should they see but Kevin and his mom! James hid the glitter behind his back.

"Hi, James! What are you hiding?" asked Kevin. "Did you buy something?"

"It's nothing," said James.

"Come on, show me."

"I can't. It's a secret," said James. "We have to go. We're in a hurry."

"A secret!" Kevin said to himself. "What kind of friends keep secrets from each other? Maybe James doesn't want to be my friend anymore."

The next day, Kevin and James did not talk to each other at all. At free time, James went to the creation station. Kevin wanted to play there too. But when he saw James, he changed his mind and went to the science center.

James looked at the paper, scissors, crayons, and glue. Somehow, the creation station did not seem like much fun anymore. He went to the reading corner instead.

On the morning of Valentine's Day, Kevin put on his red sweater. But he was not in a Valentine's Day mood. He looked at the special card he had made. I'm only going to give it to him if he tells me his secret, thought Kevin.

At that same moment, James was looking at the glittery card he had made for Kevin. I'm not even going to bring it to school, he thought. Kevin isn't my friend anymore.

James' mother kissed him good-bye. "Have fun at your party today!" she said. "And don't forget Kevin's valentine. You worked so hard on it!"

"Oh, all right," said James.

In Mrs. Fisher's room, all the kids were happy
and excited about the Valentine's Day party.
That is, all except Kevin and James. When the
time came to pass out valentines, they did not
even look at each other.

Kevin reached into his backpack for the bag of cards he brought. By accident, the special valentine flipped out and landed on the floor. It popped open and out sprang a big red heart! It said, "Happy Valentine's Day, James!"

"Wow!" said James. "Did you make that for me?"

"Sure," said Kevin. "I worked on it for two days. That's why I couldn't come over to play."

"Oh, so that's it!" said James. Suddenly, he felt much better. "I have a surprise for you, too."

When Kevin saw the special valentine James
made, he smiled for the first time in a long
time. "It has all my favorite things!" he said.

"You almost spoiled the surprise when you
caught me buying the glitter," said James.

"So that was the secret!" said Kevin.

"This is the best valentine I've ever seen."

"No, the one you made is even better," said James. "Can you show me how to make a spring later?"

"Sure," said Kevin, "if you show me how to draw a shark."

That day, at free time, Kevin and James could be found at their usual place. They had a happy Valentine's Day after all.

Hearts in Bloom

On Valentine's Day, we show our family and friends how much we like them. One way is to send cards. Another way is to give flowers. You can make a flower out of hearts to give to someone special!

You will need:

—Red, pink, and white construction paper (These are the colors of Valentine's Day. You can use different colors if you like.)
—Green construction paper
—scissors
—glue

1. Cut a long thin piece of green construction paper. This willl be the stem. Cut out two or three small hearts from the green paper, as shown. These will be leaves. Glue them to the stem.
2. Cut out a white or pink circle. Glue it to the top of the stem. Then cut out some pink and red hearts to use as petals for the flower.

Squiggle Hearts
This pretty heart decoration is also fun to make!

You will need:
—white paper
—bottle of glue
—watercolor paints and a paintbrush
—newspapers

1. Fold the paper in half and cut out a heart.

2. Spread newspapers on a table. Put the heart on the newspapers. Squeeze the glue to make thin squiggles all over your heart. Let it dry completely. (Maybe overnight.)

3. When the glue is dry, paint the whole heart with watercolors. What happens to the glued parts?

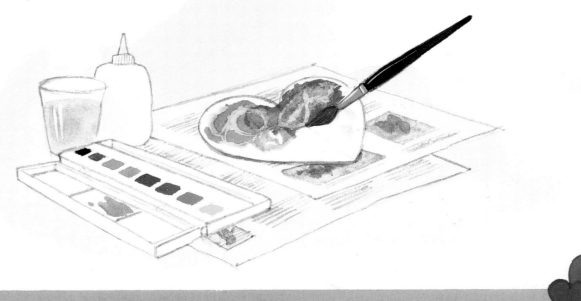

Guess the Secret Valentine

Here is a fun game to play on Valentine's Day. It is best to play this game with a large group of friends. The more, the merrier!

How to get ready:

1. Write down each player's name and put each name in an envelope. (Instead of names, you can use photos of the players.)
2. Put the envelopes in a bag or a box.

How to play:

1. All of the players sit in a circle.
2. One player pretends to be the mail carrier. That person takes an envelope out of the mail bag or mail box. Then the mail carrier describes the "secret valentine" to the other players.
3. Whoever guesses who the secret valentine is gets to be the next mail carrier.

Helpful Hints:

1. Don't start with clues that are too easy. You could say: "This valentine likes to play with blocks," or "This valentine is a good artist." If no one guesses right, then you can say, "She has brown hair."
2. Don't look at your secret valentine while you are thinking of clues!

A Valentine's Day "Pinkshake"

Sweet treats are another fun part of Valentine's Day. You can make a pink milkshake to celebrate!

You will need:

—10 ounces of frozen strawberries or raspberries
—4 cups of cold milk
—a blender (and an adult to use it!)

Scoop the frozen berries and pour the milk into the blender. Ask an adult to blend them until the mixture is smooth. This delicious recipe will feed about five valentines!

Can you think of other pink or red food to eat or drink on Valentine's Day?